ISBN: 978-1-956076-09-7

PROOFREADING and CREATIVE DIRECTION by NaBeela Washington
COVER ART and CREATIVE DIRECTION by Ivana Jarmon
GUEST EDITING by Mel Sherrer
PROOFREADING by Nia Brass
COVER MODEL Destiny Brady

A Black writer and art collector, NaBeela Washington holds a Master's in Creative Writing and English from Southern New Hampshire University and a Bachelor's in Visual Advertising from The University of Alabama at Birmingham. She is the Founder of *Lucky Jefferson*.

Ivana Jarmon, a Chicago-based photographer, is driven by a profound passion for storytelling. Her work delves into themes that authentically capture and reflect the essence of Blackness, exploring the realms of vulnerability and celebrating the inherent beauty of the Black experience.

Mel Sherrer (She/Her) received her B.F.A. from Hollins University in Roanoke, VA. and her M.F.A. from Converse University in Spartanburg, SC. Mel is the author of Vice Grip (ABP, 2021) and she has poetry published in Poet Lore, Zone 3 Press, Storm Cellar, SWWIM, Interim, and others. She currently teaches courses in Performance Literature and Poetry, and serves as the Pop Culture Editor for Sage Cigarettes Magazine. Find her work and more information at MelSherrer.com.

Publication of *Lucky Jefferson* is made possible through community support.

Donate or submit to *Lucky Jefferson* on our website: luckyjefferson.com.

FOREWORD

As a child in rural Georgia, I knew the bends and brambles of the woods around my home better than I knew the hallways of the grade school I attended. I remember the lanky, fat-bellied deer prancing through the underbrush. I remember the depth of the darkness in the forest at night. I remember watching my mother fishing, and later taking up the practice myself. Most of all, I remember the freedom of eating after hours of sweat, work, and patience. I remember the freedom of the wilderness and the sustenance provided there. Those moments in the woods, on the creek bank, taught me that the most free a Black girl might ever feel is within the unpredictability of the untamed, natural world.

I know Black creatives who hunt, fish, homestead, are homeopaths, forage, cultivate, butcher, bushcraft, and cure. What these people have in common is a sense of confidence, self-sufficiency, pure love for the land, and a significant sense of reclamation. We have reclaimed our relationship with the bygone skills necessary to interact with the land our fore parents were forced to work in and our collective, literary legacy.

Let this collection mark a departure from stereotypes of Black Americans outside solely to work or be worked, and the convalescence of Black people's relationship with wilderness. It is overdue for Black writers who are writing about their experiences engaging with nature and the environment to be acknowledged as Naturalists, Rusticists, Environmentalists, Eco-Poets, and Transcendentalists. These stories point at soil beneath nails, at hands that till, sow, and sweep leaves from the cave floor, at wanderers who kneel to pull from the stream, and explorers who set up camp, and make fire before nightfall.

Mel Sherrer
Guest Editor

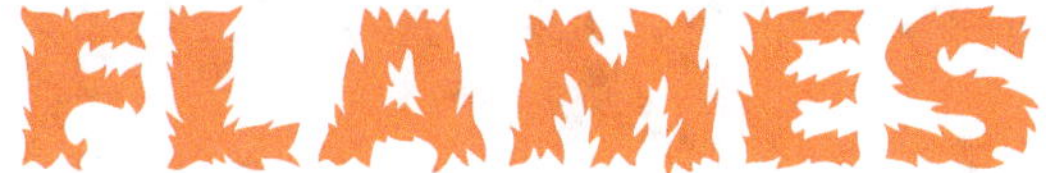

FLAMES

HYPNOSIS

Dylan Connell

The moth grew cold by the bed of the sea. A long fruitless search was coming to an end. When the sun had been high, the moth roamed the warm earth following the tale of summers sweetest honey. Still, before he could discover if the story was truth or fiction, the sun fell once again, deep into the empty sea. And the moth—trapped in the frigid air of a night whose clouds blocked the moon—froze into numbness.

Hopeless in this struggle, the moth gave into exhaustion and rested his tired wings. It was in this very moment that a distant flicker ignited on the horizon. The spark set the stage; the coast became a theater for dancing shadows. So it was, with this discovery of light, the moth was rejuvenated.

Thus, despite feeling moments ago that his wings contained not a beat left within them. The moth—embracing his new purpose—fluttered softly towards the light and the comforting embrace of warmth.

Forgetting once again that the cold almost swallowed him. The moth arrived at the flame of a single lantern.

As the target approached, he found himself transfixed, unable to look away as though under hypnosis. With no way to resist that mesmerizing figure, there was only one remaining action for the moth to carry out. That was, to run headfirst into the glass whose presence he could not perceive.

The flame was indifferent; it did nothing but consume the wax which fed it. The moth however, yearned more and more for the golden body of life and light. The cycle continued this way for hours. That was, until the moth found an opening in the top of the lantern's construction. With his vision realized, he descended upon blinding desire with an open heart.

But the moth was not greeted with the warmth it longed for. Instead, its wings ignited, and its stiff body plummeted into a trap of liquid wax. Even the effort of kicking legs did nothing but spin the moth deeper into thick elixir.

Finally, in a last cruel joke, strawberry red clouds kissed the horizon, and the sun rose. The candle was blown out and the wax thickened. Imprinting the moths struggle for all to see.

PAST TIMES (1997) BY KERRY JAMES MARSHALL

Ellen June Wright

As video from Atlanta and another
    Black man's murder chills me with grief,
I long for a moment in Marshall's America.

Black is the fit female skiing on the lake
    and Black is the care-free boater cruising by
and black is the golfer slicing his ball over the water
    and Black is the young girl playing croquet
and Black is the woman opening her picnic basket
    on a red and white checkered cloth
and Black is the boy lounging on the lawn;
    everyone's carefree in summer whites
and even the chocolate-black Rottweiler
    is content as *it's just my imagination*
and *mind on my money* lyrics float up
    on banners from dueling black boomboxes
into the pastoral air as blue birds crown
    this bliss and the projects are a distant truth

and the lake couldn't be bluer if we were free
    and this day out was not imagination but a memory.

SEMPER FI IS TO EMINENT DOMAIN AS SANCTUARY IS TO VERTIGO

Leslie McIntosh

Shifting in the photo
that is also a map.
Two dimensional
but strangely erect.
Not distorted yet. Wind
in the ribcage, wind
in the marrow. Charted
from exterior view
because the inside
was a hoarder's nest,
my self on the floor
lined up, in pieces.
I loved me that way
until the Army came
banging. I was alone.
Mom was at work.
They blew up the door.

Smoke and debris
flew so surely,
it must have been
our apartment spiraling
all this time. Otherwise,
how could me be
casually smithereens
here, at home,
in my own business,
right? Me—mixed
perfectly with the detritus
strewn across the tender
order I shared
with my mother.
They swept the area.
I stood there. I said
nothing. I shook
all their hands
before they filed away.
I nudged bits of me
with the toes of my
dirty boots. Discreetly,
of course,
you know?

RENDITION: FANNING THE FIRE

Olatunde Osinaike

Where the broken invest, the law enters, plots its split.
Remember when hearts had water and light? Room and vision?

      Memories hearts couldn't forgo, the land I'd envisioned
      and what I can never say about its dark.

I can tell you so little about the dark
without mentioning the light that resides.

      How could I fail to mention how light resides,
      with no permission, no instructions.

Power prefers no permission, no instructions
for its aftermath and that's how I was introduced to my country.

      Speaking of ruin, I've never met a country I liked
      more than the spirit of belief among its people.

With your spirit, give me a reason to believe in people.
Broken now, the law we once knew – away, my own.

MOVING TO MIRAMAR

Kyle Williams

Bald cypress cover,
cleavage-less Sun.
Collected palm water
slosh the painted toes of
mud-baked slacker gators.
Lime on the swamp lawn while
dragonfly HOAs buzz around
their ancient tenants.
JawSnap.

THINKING OF YOU

Jonathan Chibuike Ukah

The mountain appears before me,
to show me how to ignite a fire
and I can see through its top,
flat like my father's new mahogany table,
built like fine, smooth glass.
I feel I can jump on it and sing
of my triumph over pain and sorrow,
the gentle touch under my sole
that is all I can think of you.

Fire sucked my blood and licked my bones;
the mountain towered over the sky;
I tucked into rugged holes, pines of trees
and littered pieces of broken glass,
and a cluster of birds dump,
a sharpened scythe to drive smoke away
almost made me forget to get to the top
and seeing how close to Heaven the mountain is,
and that's how I think your love has been.

You are my fire, my flame,
and I'm yet learning to put you up,
to set you up like a bomb, a cocktail of grenades,
either in the morning or in the dark,
and as the stars sneak out to parade in the sky,
you will rise into a brilliant, yellow pyramid.

SPELL MISSISSIPPI WITHOUT SINGING IT

Jasmine Barnes

hear(e)
the only music
is dirge or anthem

the confederacy
southern gothic pledge
meticulously woven into state flag
skillful pain-staking embroidery
longing for the casualties of crusade

what other deaths does one die living under such a promise?

we stopped to pick flowers on the side of the road
heavy and fragrant with summer humidity
kneeling and standing
two holy women
bowing reverent in prayer
hoping the blossoms
might camouflage us

as benevolent creatures
too beautiful
to harm

GARDEN REPRISE

Olivia Dorsey Peacock

i entered the outside.
buried fingers in
wayward leaves, acknowledged
horsetail, nettle, clover, crabgrass
twisted
      barren throats, plunged flesh
      into contrary thorns, draped
      insect corpses with crimson,
      sacrificed an exhale,
      pulsated muscle
            and still, roots did not give way.

LITANY FOR DEEP & SHAKY BREATH

psykhe rietveld

i am a blue ribbon pumpkin &
the farmer growing it &
the county fair gawking
delightedly at my circumference.
i am alive.

and then i am consuming
the consumer before the consumer
consumes me and i put the consumer
on dinner rolls.
i am alive.

and then lay my big body
in the flood before it reaches the village
and in my leisure, i've become
a dark, glistening dam.
i am alive.

and then my mom calls me after a month of not hearing me,
and she tells me she is so happy
that my laugh sounds like mine.
she tells me this for an hour.
i am alive.

and then i turn my face
to the too-hot sun
and let her dry the tears off my crying face.
i smell summer and remember that
i am alive.

in the crisp open air,
i find delight in the wind
letting the breeze guide my footsteps
for outside i am safe and
i am alive.

my lungs stay full of air
drawn in for wheezing laughter.
thank god for the atmosphere,
i survive because
i am alive.

What common themes have you noticed so far?
Pick a poem (or story) from pages 14-33 & continue writing it.

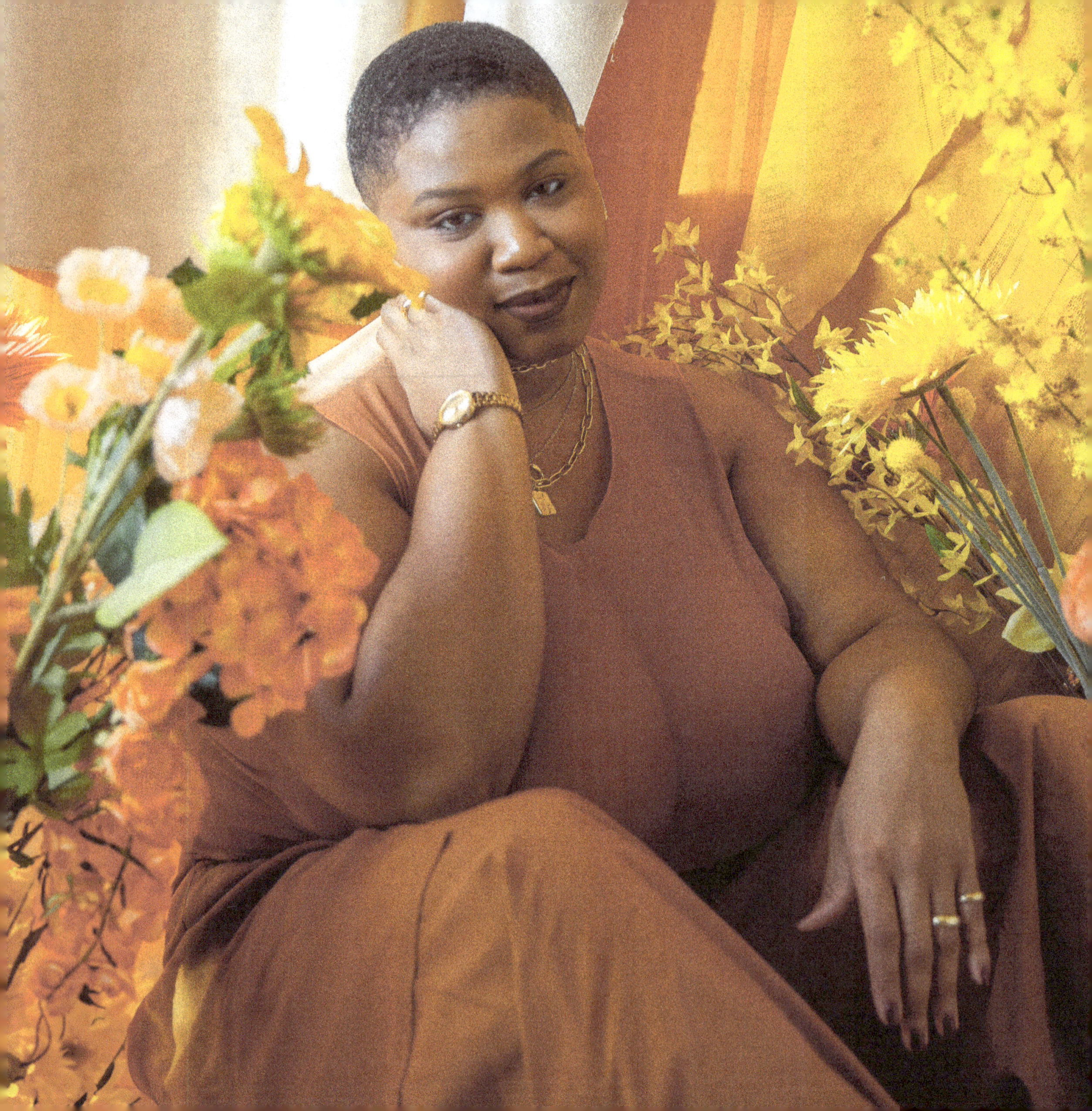

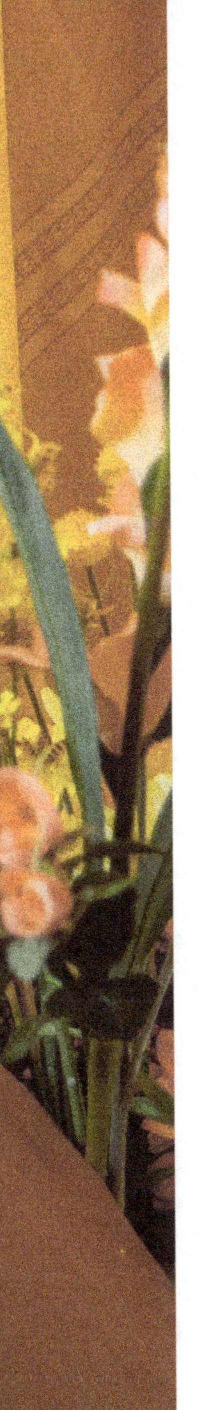

LEARN ABOUT
How We Make Fire's Cover Model

Destiny Brady is a Chicago-raised Southsider who engages art, design, journalism, exhibition design, farming, and curatorial practice to create opportunities for like-minded people of many ages to learn and grow together.

Countering the lack of robust and nuanced representation of Black people and their experiences in many institutions, Brady aims to highlight love, legacy, happiness, kindness, intelligence, heritage, ease, and joy. Since receiving her architecture degree from the University of Wisconsin-Milwaukee, Brady centers the question of "What if we were all wiped from this earth, what would be left of us?" to help guide her practice.

She has held a residency with the National Public Housing Museum, Chicago Art Department, and Contextos Gallery in Chicago. Her work has been featured in The Black Joy Project, Culture ICON, and Braided Magazine. Since completing her McMullan Arts Leadership internship in the Art Institute of Chicago's Architecture and Design curatorial department, Brady is following her internship with a Masters in Curating Contemporary Design at Kingston University in London, United Kingdom. Her education and career pursuits are aimed toward her own architecture and design practice The Kids Are From The Future (TIKA Studios).

SUBMIT TO LUCKY JEFFERSON

Lucky Jefferson's mission is simple: we publish social change.

And our vision is to see books reimagined to center the modern reader.

Founded in 2018, *Lucky Jefferson* is an award-winning nonprofit, literary journal, and publisher that reimagines books by creating interactive and collaborative community experiences that center the writer and artist and cultivate inclusion and representation in contemporary literature.

Lucky Jefferson is proud to feature poets and writers who have never been published, marginalized perspectives, and those who sought to pursue writing later in life.

Learn more + consider submitting at: **luckyjefferson.com**

FOLLOW US

📷 @lucky_jefferson

🐦 @_luckyjefferson

f @luckyjeffersonlit

STRIKE A POSE

take a selfie
with your copy of
How We Make Fire
and tag us!

HASHTAGSSSS

use #HowWeMakeFire, #Awake6,
or #LJSQUAD to follow the convo